Floor Planning

A Step-By-Step Guide to Maximizing Your Living Space

Missy Miller

DIY Skoolie Guide Press

DIY SKOOLIE FLOOR PLANNING

ISBN: 978-1-7343976-1-1

Printed in the United States of America

DISCLAIMER

These are not architectural design plans. The plans may have to be modified or adjusted depending on your bus. We—the author and the team at DIY Skoolie Guide— are not responsible for any mishaps while using these plans. The reader/builder is accepting all responsibility for all risks during the construction when using these plans.

Table of Contents

INTRODUCTION 7

CHAPTER 1   It All Starts with You...8

CHAPTER 2   Get Ideas for Your Floor Plan 10

CHAPTER 3   Choose a Design Tool for Your Floor Plan 12

CHAPTER 4   Know Your Measurements.......................................13

CHAPTER 5   Windows and Doors...17

CHAPTER 6   Wheel Wells Influence Design 21

CHAPTER 7   Storage Space..23

CHAPTER 8   Placing Your Tanks...26

CHAPTER 9   The Bathroom...28

CHAPTER 10 The Kitchen and Appliances 31

CHAPTER 11 The Bedrooms...35

CHAPTER 12 The Living Area..40

CHAPTER 13 Power 43

CHAPTER 14 Heating and Cooling...45

CHAPTER 15 Planning for Your Wellbeing.................................47

CHAPTER 16 The Extras 50

CHAPTER 17 Design Your Skoolie Floor Plan 54

APPENDIX 57

Questions to Ask Yourself Before Planning a Skoolie Design 59

Helpful Standard Measurements...63

RV Dealer Notes 66

Furniture to Reuse or Recycle...67

Appliance List...68

Graph Paper...69

INTRODUCTION

Skoolie popularity is on the rise! With shows like Tiny House Nation showing skoolies as an option for tiny living and the accounts on Instagram growing daily, skoolies are becoming desired by many.

Taking the dream from inspirational videos or photos to an actual plan is where the challenges start. Many people give up after making several costly mistakes. Even more people are living in their skoolie and making changes to the design because the layout is not working for them. Don't let that be you! You are on the right track by using books like this to get a plan in place.

In this book, you are going to answer question after question. These questions are going to help you get a real look at your needs, wants, and must-haves inside your skoolie. I am going to help you plan the skoolie that will fit your needs and your family.

This book has been designed to be both instructional and functional. I have integrated a workbook into the text so that you can answer these questions as you go. I encourage you to do this. Don't just answer these questions in your mind. Easy come, easy go! Instead, take the time to really think about them and write down your responses. By the time you finish this book, you will have a very detailed list of what you need, what you want, and what you cannot live without in your skoolie.

That's invaluable!

Once you have the questions answered, we are going to step-by-step through the floor planning process. At the end of this book, you will have a floor plan created. If at any time you decide that you want to reach out to a professional, I am available for floor planning consults and will answer any of your questions.

Contact me at Missy@diyskoolieguide.com for more information.

Pro Tip: *Go spend a few nights in a skoolie before buying one. You will be able to gather ideas about what works and doesn't work for you.*

CHAPTER 1
It All Starts with You

Are you anything like me and as soon as you get your school bus home, you can't wait to design the floor plan? One of the things I love about school bus conversions is that I get to make the space fit my needs.

Now it is your turn to take that empty metal box and design it to fit you, yourneeds, and your wants.

Do you like to plan and make lists? If so, you are going to love this book. If not, DON'T close the book just yet. I promise that I will make this as painless as possible for you—and I also promise that no matter how much you may think you don't need this process, you do.

Imagine Your Life in a Skoolie

If you came to me for a floor planning consultation, one of the first things I would tell you to do is to close your eyes and envision yourself waking up in the morning.

What are the first things you are going to do?

Do you grab your phone off the nightstand and scroll through social media? Are your slippers nearby and you slide your feet in and head to the bathroom? Do you stumble to the coffee pot and go get in the shower?

Picture yourself moving throughout an entire weekday and a weekend. What do you like to do in the evenings? What do you do when you are stressed? When you can't sleep?

It's important to see yourself moving through your life so that you know what you need to have on hand in your skoolie.

When converting my first skoolie, I used the front of the bus as my bedroom. I didn't have a place to go in the morning to drink my coffee in the quiet. Now, if you don't know much about me at that time, I had seven children ages 3-13. I needed my morning coffee quiet time to keep me sane and them safe! However, because I didn't think about this before I made my skoolie floor plan, I had to get creative. On rainy days, it meant me getting up early (that alone caused some problems) and the kids staying in their beds until I could swallow my coffee quickly in quiet. On sunny days, it meant me finding a place outside away from noise to start my day healthy. Depending on where we were, sometimes this was not practical.

And to think—it all could have been avoided if I had realized this ahead of time!

Answering Questions

Over the next several chapters, you will find many questions to ask yourself. These questions are designed to help you recognize what you, your partner, and/or your kids need in your skoolie to stay healthy mentally, physically, emotionally, and spiritually. These questions will also focus on the practical side of things, such as where do you want your kitchen to be and where you're going to mount your tanks under your bus.

You can find a comprehensive list of all of these questions at the back of the book in the appendix section.

Once you have answered all of these questions, you will have a pretty good snapshot of what you need, what you want, and what you can't live without in your skoolie. Trust me, you definitely want to know this ahead of time.

Otherwise, you will find out the hard way!

CHAPTER 2
Get Ideas for Your Floor Plan

You will design your floor plan around the things that you need and the things that are important to you. But how do you want your floor plan to look? How will it all come together?

If you were building a stick-and-brick house, the contractor would ask you to take a look at several floor plans and tell him what you do and don't like about each plan. Well, you are converting a bus into your home, so this process shouldn't be any different. So, go on a search for skoolie floor plans!

Where can you find good examples of skoolie floor plans? Look on Pinterest boards, do a Google search, check out YouTube and across the web for different skoolie ideas. You may want to add a feature from one plan and another feature from a different plan. This will help you to come up with your own unique design.

Add links to your favorite floor plans here:

Take Some Tours

Take a trip to a local RV dealer and walk through the RVs, making notes of what you like and don't like. Be sure to bring a tape measure so you can measure items to get an idea of how long a couch is or how wide the closet should be.

As you are looking at the different plans, write down your thoughts, ideas, and things you do and don't like. Think about the way your doors will open, the places you will store things, and how much space you will actually need in certain areas.

Another suggestion is to go visit tiny house events. Due to the popularity of skoolies, you are sure to find more than one to walk through. If not, get in a Facebook Group and see if there are some skoolie owners who will let you tour theirs. You will find that the skoolie community is welcoming, encouraging, and accepting. Have fun and enjoy dreaming about living and traveling in your skoolie.

Pro Tip: *If you want to shortcut your process, we invite you to come check out our website at DIYskoolieguide.com. You will find many helpful resources there, and you can even book a one-on-one planning consultation with me.*

RV Dealer Notes

What I liked:

What I didn't like:

Measurements taken:

CHAPTER 3
Choose a Design Tool for Your Floor Plan

There are a lot of fancy design tools out there you can use to design your floor plan. There are softwares for your computer and apps for your phone. There are free options, and there are paid options.

However, none of them are for me. My personal favorite design tool is graph paper and a pencil. I make each square represent 12 inches. Then, I draw a rectangle on the paper with the correct dimensions of my bus.

What size bus are you thinking of purchasing? In the appendix, I have included some graph paper for you to print off. Pick the size you need and print off three copies.

If you're a little more high-tech than that, I don't blame you. So, here are a few programs that I have seen or heard of people in the skoolie community using:

- Home Styler: http://www.homestyler.com/designer This is FREE and fun to use.
- Sketch Up: http://www.sketchup.com/ This is a FREE 3D modeling program. There are a few videos on YouTube that will lessen the learning curve if you want to play around with this program.
- Floor Planner: http://www.floorplanner.com/ This has FREE and paid options. Room Sketcher: http://www.roomsketcher.com/ This starts at $49 per year.

Things to Think About

Before you grab a pencil and graph paper or open the design app, you will want to take the time to answer all the questions in this book. Over the next several chapters, I will take you through each component of your floor plan. I have also provided a comprehensive list of questions at the back of the book (see *Questions to Ask Yourself BEFORE Planning a Skoolie Design* in the appendix). Answer these questions honestly, because it will help you narrow down your needs, wants, and cannot-live-without items.

I can't overstate the importance of this step. This is where you're going to really think about what you want from your skoolie. By thoroughly answering ALL of the questions, you will save yourself a ton of bustrations (frustrations caused by converting or living in a bus).

Think about what you want in the back of the bus and move forward. The point of envisioning yourself in your bus is to think about how you will live, play, and work in your bus. Be honest with yourself! What are the things you can't live without? Be creative! This is going to be your HOME, or a HOME away from

HOME, so make sure you are really comfortable with your design.

CHAPTER 4
Know Your Measurements

When you're planning your floor plan, you're going to plan down to the inch in order to get the absolute most out of all 270 square feet or less of living space. Below, we've listed many of the standard measurements you want to be aware of. We've also listed a few other things you need to take into consideration.

Wall Thickness

When you're accounting for the sizes of everything, don't forget to account for wall thickness! Remember, you're going to be building walls throughout your bus. You need to consider both the dimensions of your studs and the wall material itself. If you leave out the thickness of your walls, it will add up. Believe me, I know!

At this point, if you do not know what material will be used for the bus wall, just add in the thickness of your studs. Typically stud walls use 2x2s, while the width of a 2x2, however, is actually 1 ½ inches. To cover the walls, lauan is often used (pronounced "loo-on"). The lauan sheets are about ½ inch thick. When you add the studs and the lauan plywood on both sides, the thickness will come to 2 ½ inches. Do you see how that can make a difference in your plan depending on how many interior walls you have?

What are the measurements of the studs you're using?

What will you use to cover your walls?

What are the dimensions of those materials?

Clearance from Ceiling to Floor

Think about how much head space you're going to have—and how much you're going to need. How tall is the tallest person who is going to be living or traveling in your skoolie? The depth of your flooring will affect your clearance. Some floorings are thicker than others.

How tall is the tallest person who is going to be living or traveling on your skoolie? If you need extra head room, you can also consider doing a roof raise.

The Shower Valve

Another measurement that is often missed is allowing for the shower valve. The wall that the shower valve will go onto will need to be 4 inches deep to hold the valve.

Doors

Allow room for your doors to open without coming in contact with the AC unit or ceiling vent. You also want to make sure that you have room to open your washer/dryer, cabinet, and refrigerator doors.

How much clearance do your doors require?

Bedroom:

Cabinets:

Washer/Dryer:

Refrigerator:

Other_____

Windows

Your windows will be an important element of your floor plan. Make sure to know the length of the windows. Most school bus windows measure 2 ½ feet across.

When placing the stud walls, make sure not to have a stud in the middle of any window you plan on keeping.

Keep in mind how the bus will look from the outside. Do you want someone seeing stud walls through your bus windows?

Pro Tip: *There are times when you can shorten or lengthen a space just so the stud can go between the windows.*

In the next chapter, I will talk about how to determine which windows you want to keep and what to do about the windows you aren't keeping.

What are the measurements of your windows?

Furniture

When designing a skoolie, give careful consideration to the kinds of furniture that needs to be brought into the bus. Do you have your grandma's wardrobe that you must fit into the bus? Or maybe your mom gave you a table that just has to find a place in your new home. Because this furniture is not going to be built into the bus, you must get the measurements of these pieces and add them to the floor plan so that they can be built around.

One of the ways to save on your skoolie budget is to recycle your current belongings. I have seen people use dressers as vanities and kitchen cabinets. I have seen pots used as sinks. These choices save money and bring an eclectic personal style to the skoolie. (For more information on how much you should budget for your conversion, check out our *Cost of Conversion* book, which can be found at diyskoolieguide.com) When adding your personal furniture into your build, it is important to know the measurements of each item ahead of time to save money and time in the future.

What existing furniture will you be bringing into your skoolie? List the items on the next page and record the dimensions of each piece.

Furniture to Reuse or Recycle

Items	Room Placement	Measurements	Notes

CHAPTER 5
Windows and Doors

When designing your floor plan, you will need to decide how many windows you would like to keep, replace, or cover up. Some clients want to keep as many windows as possible to let in all the natural light. I totally understand this, as I don't like being in a dark, closed room for long periods of time. Let's face it—it makes me sad and moody. The windows you're starting with are old-school bus windows, so they are not insulated. Keeping them will affect the temperature in your skoolie.

A way to keep the windows and reduce the negative effects is to keep the windows that are in the correct spot—meaning the windows that are actually useful where they are. For instance, two windows across from each other will provide cross ventilation. Another window may offer the best view. An incorrect spot would be where a window is going to be useless. Some people leave windows in a closet!

Recommendations for Windows

- Keep the full windows behind and across from the couch.
- Keep half windows behind the kitchen cabinets. (The cabinet height is higher than the bottom window.)
- Keep two windows on each side in the master bedroom.
- Keep one window on each side if you have a hallway.
- Remove all windows in the bathroom.
- Remove the windows in the kid's area, OR keep the top halves only.
- Cover all windows that are behind walls. (You can get video instructions for this by subscribing to our online DIY Skoolie Masterclass.)

Replacing Windows

If you decide on a roof raise, you have the option to raise the roof below the window and keep the original windows. Another option is to remove all the windows, cover them with sheet metal, and add RV windows where you would like them.

RV windows can be purchased, tinted, and double paned. The cost of replacing the bus windows with RV windows will increase your overall skoolie budget.

I recommend doing this if you get a roof raise and are going into extreme temperatures.

It will be extremely important to have a detailed floor plan before you begin the roof raise when you are replacing the windows.

You can replace the windows if you don't do a roof raise. Again, just have to have a detailed plan before removing the windows.

Pro Tip: *There is no wiggle room once the walls start going up. If you have to add inches in one place, you will lose them in another. It's a great idea to allow an extra inch here and there just in case.*

Mark Off the Windows You're Keeping

Once you decide what windows you are keeping, grab some blue painter tape. Place a piece of tape on each window that will get covered up by a wall. This way you can visually tell if you like the design and, if you are not home, your partner will not cover up a window that should be left alone.

Which windows are you keeping?

If you are replacing windows, where are you going to purchase the new RV windows? (If you're considering more than one place, record the price comparisons below.)

Bus Doors

The number of doors your bus will have depends on the style and model you buy. If you get a short to mid-size bus, you will most likely have a back door at the rear, a side door toward the back on the passenger side, and a front passenger door.

If you purchase a rear engine bus, you will have a front passenger door and a side door either in the middle on the driver's side or passenger side.

Front engine buses will have a rear door and a front passenger door.

So, you could have a bus with two or three doors, and they can be in places that will alter your floor plan design.

Door Placement

When you start designing your floor plan, you want to think about the design in relation to the placement of the doors.

Some floor plans that utilize the side door in the bathroom. This way, you can enter the bathroom from outside the bus if you have sandy kids or muddy dogs, which helps keep the mess less in the skoolie. The side door can also be used as an access for people to empty a compost toilet from the outside.

When I designed my floor plan, I specifically designed it around the doors. I had a mid-size bus with a rear door and a passenger door at the back. My purpose was to vacation in the skoolie and use it at tiny home shows. I wanted my guests to be able to enter from the front and exit from the side. In addition, while vacationing, I wanted to be able to lie in bed, open both doors, and take scenic photos. (I love those IG photos of wonderful views taken by people relaxing while looking out the door. Don't you?)

On occasion, I see people completely block off all rear doors because they want to secure the bus. Of course this is an option, but I would caution you to keep one rear door accessible or be sure that you have an egress window in case of emergency.

How many bus doors does your bus have, and where are they?

What are the measurements for each door?

What is the distance from the edge of each door to the adjacent wall(s)?

Do you want to keep the back door accessible?

Are you keeping the front bus door or using an RV Door?

If you have a side door, what is the distance from each side of the door to the front and rear of the bus?

Would you like to have a side entrance into the skoolie?

Would you like to empty the compost toilet from the outside?

How important is it for you to keep access to the doors?

How many egress exits do you have?

CHAPTER 6
Wheel Wells Influence Design

One thing every school bus converter wants to do is to remove the wheel wells. I have done this on ONE bus, and I do not recommend it unless you have a fabrication team. Take a look at RV accidents where the tire has blown and the damage it causes to the interior of the RV. There is a reason the wheel well is there!

Pro Tip: *Some buses that are 2007 or newer have no wheel wells!*

So, how are you going to design around them?

The wheel wells have to be taken into consideration during the floor plan. Think about what you can build over or on top of them. You can put almost anything on them: compost toilets, tubs, couches, kitchen counters, closets, and more!

If you decide to place a sink or tub on the wheel wells, be sure you can run your PEX pipe in the wall and then down to where it is not directly above the tire. The tub drain is best placed in front of the tire, in my opinion. Due to the ceiling clearance, a shower cannot go over the wheel well unless you raise the roof.

In addition, some wheel wells protrude into the hallway. Make sure if you are sitting a washer on top of the wheel well that you have room to open the door. You would not want to build two closets with doors across from each other if the wheel wells are deep, because the closet doors will hit each other when opened.

Some people have created a side-aisle skoolie and have to use the wheel well as a step. This works great, if you are comfortable with it.

Several items you can place on top of the wheel wells include:

- Undercounter refrigerator
- Washer/dryer
- Utility closet or clothes closet
- Pets area—dog crate, cat tree/hideout, litter box
- Pantry or kitchen cabinets
- Custom couch
- Bookshelf
- Compost Toilet*
- Sink
- Tub, as long as the drain will have room to drain under the bus without being near the tire.

* Placing a toilet on top of the wheel well can be done, but it is not advised it if it is a water flush toilet.

What are the dimensions of the wheel wells in your bus?

How far is it from the last wheel well to the back of the bus?

How far is it from the front wheel well to the front of the bus?

What is the distance between the wheel wells front to back and side to side?

CHAPTER 7
Storage Space

One of the main questions about living on a skoolie is whether or not there is enough storage space. My reply is a resounding YES! The trick is to look for ways that you can make items serve more than one purpose. This is especially true for furniture.

Couch Storage

One popular design is a couch that covers the wheel well and also doubles as storage. Some people choose to bring in their own couch. Others like a futon that folds down into a bed. Personally, I think the couch-storage idea is the best option of all.

If you are wanting a couch that has both storage underneath and functions as a bed, you can subscribe to our online DIY Skoolie Masterclass, which gives step-by-step video instructions on exactly how to do that.

Are you going to custom-build a couch with storage space in it?

What will you store in your couch?

Bedroom Storage

You will have several options for storage in the bedroom, including closets, if you plan for them in your floor plan. I suggest customizing your bed so that you have storage space underneath. Some skoolie owners divide the storage space under the bed so that some of it is accessible from inside of the bus and some of it is accessible from outside of the bus. For more ideas on bed designs and which kind will best fit your storage needs, see *Chapter 11: The Bedroom.*

Do you want a cabinet on each side of the bed, or are you going to save space and crawl over your partner to get out of bed?

Do you want storage underneath the bed?

Do you want room on the sides of the bed to walk around, or would you prefer having extra storage space?

Do you want a closet or storage in the master bedroom?

Do you need a closet or toy storage in a kid's room?

In the Kitchen

Your kitchen should be equipped with ample storage space for all of your kitchen needs. It's a small space but planning wisely will go a long way. You can install upper and lower cabinets and shelving.

Keep in mind that this will likely be a multi-purpose space. Maybe the kitchen table also needs to be used as a work desk or sewing area. In some designs, I have seen a flip up countertop to extend the space when needed and fold downwhen not in use.

What are the pieces of furniture you will use for more than one purpose? List the items and what they will be used for:

Garage

Some skoolie owners want a garage area. This is an area where they can store items and get to them from outside the bus. Many people also leave access under the bed that they can reach from the back door.

Do you want a garage area?

What will you be storing there?

How much space, if any, do you want in the back of the bus?

CHAPTER 8
Placing Your Tanks

There are three different kinds of tanks that you will be installing into your bus. Each one will add a lot to your quality of life on the road. When doing your floor plan, it's important to know what size tanks you will be using and where you will install them.

Freshwater Tank

A freshwater tank is a tank that holds drinkable water. The water can be used to shower, wash dishes, drink, and flush the toilet. Freshwater tanks are available in different sizes. The most popular are 30-gallon, 50-gallon, and 100-gallon tanks. When thinking about what size you want to install into your bus, consider how often the bus will be connected to city water.

Think about where it will be installed. When possible, it is best to install this tank on the inside of the bus to reduce the chances of the water freezing during the winter. Some great places to install a freshwater tank are under the master bed, under a couch, or even in the kitchen area.

Gray Tank

A gray tank is a tank that holds the wastewater from sinks and the shower. (It's black in color, but it's called a gray tank because of the type of water it holds.) When deciding on what size gray tank to purchase, think about how often you want to dump and how many people are on the bus using water and taking showers each day. Gray tanks come in sizes ranging from 23 gallons up to 65 gallons. Just make sure to purchase one that will fit the space where you have planned to placed the tank. Always know your measurements.

In my bus, I had one gray tank connected to the kitchen sink and bathroom sink and another gray tank just for the shower. Having more than one gray tank is a good idea if you're boondocking or just don't want to empty the tanks as often.

Black Tank

A black tank is a tank that holds the contents from the toilet. Usually, it is located directly under the toilet. Black tanks come in the sizes ranging from 23 gallons up to 65 gallons, just like the gray tanks.

Get the Measurements

When determining the sizes of the tanks you need. Measure the lengths, heights, and depths of the places where the tanks are going to be secured. Be aware of the wheel wells. If you are using a water flush toilet, make sure the tanks will fit right under the toilet. Sometimes the exhaust system or an axle may interfere with tank placement. Believe me, you do NOT want to purchase a tank and get ready to install it just to find out it will not fit.

Placing the Tanks

For easy access, install the water pump, freshwater tank, and water heater near the back door. I recommend storing them under the master bed. When installing the freshwater tank, I recommend placing it on the driver's side for easier access to the freshwater fill.

For ease of filling the freshwater tank and dumping the gray and black tanks, place all the tanks on the driver's side. Most of the time, this is the side that the dump station will be on when in a campground.

How much freshwater will you need?

Where are you going to store your freshwater tank?

How many gray tanks do you need?

Where will the gray tank(s) be placed under the bus?

Will you need a black tank?

Where will the black tank be placed under the bus?

What size hot water heater do you want?

Where are you going to put the hot water heater?

CHAPTER 9
The Bathroom

Once you know where the water tanks are going to go, you can plan out the bathroom.

In order to get the best dimensions for the bathroom, I recommend taking a bucket and sitting on it to figure out where you want the toilet to be. Then, you can easily measure exactly how much space you will need in the bathroom.

Remember, you never want to hit your knees on the sink while sitting down or your butt on a shelf when pulling up your pants.

The questions below will help you formulate the best layout, design, and function you need for your skoolie bathroom.

Placement

Think about where in you bus you want to put your bathroom. Do you want it to be on one side or span the entire width of the bus? If you have it going across the bus, the toilet and vanity could be on the passenger side and the shower could be on the driver's side. This would allow you to have two doors going into the bathroom—one to enter from the front and one to enter from the bedroom area.

A Couple Things to Remember

The shower valve

Don't forget that the wall that the shower valve will go onto will need to be 4 inches deep to hold the valve. Make sure to mark where you want it to go on your floor plan.

Proximity to tanks

Keep in mind that if you move your bathroom or kitchen sink on your floor plan, you will want to go back under your bus and make sure there is room for your gray and black tanks in the new spot.

Where are you going to place the mirror?

Will the light be in the ceiling or over the mirror?

How many electrical outlets will you need in the bathroom?

Will you leave a window in the bathroom?

Are you going to install a bathroom vent fan?

What size vanity do you need?

Do you want a tub/shower or just a shower?

What size shower/tub do you want?

What materials will you use for the tub/shower area? (tile, tin, RV surround, etc.)

Where do you want to place the bus bathroom? One side or across both sides?

What type of toilet are you going to use?

How much space do you need to get ready in the mornings?

Where will you store dirty laundry?

Do you need a storage or linen closet?

Do you want a trashcan in the bathroom?

Standard Bathroom Measurements

Bathroom Side-Aisle:
  Large: 6' 6 ½" x 4' 4½" (W x D)
  Standard: 5' 9"x 3' ½" (W x D)
Bathroom, both sides of the bus:
  6' 7" x 2' 9 ½" (W x D)
Wet-bath:
  3' 5 ½" x 2' (W x D)
Compost or RV Toilet:
  24" x 24" (W x D)
Vanity:
  18" x 34.5" x 24" or 24" x 24" x 34. 5" (W x H x D)
  (This can also be custom designed)
Vessel Sink:
  13-16" x 13-16" x 4-6" (L x W x H)
White Porcelain Rectangle Sink:
  14"-17" x 18"-21" x 5-¾" (L x W x D)
White Ceramic Rectangular Vessel Bathroom Sink:
  18-23" x 14.25" x 4.31" (L xW x D)
RV Shower:
  40" x 24" or 36" x 36" (W x D)
RV Tub:
  40" x 24" (W x D)

CHAPTER 10
The Kitchen and Appliances

When living in 270 square feet or less of living space, more than cooking is going to happen in the kitchen. When designing your kitchen, think of all the purposes it will need to serve.

For instance, if you like to bake and cook, maybe you need more countertop space. Will there be special appliances that need to be stored in the kitchen? For me, I like to make room for my Kitchen Aid Mixer. I love baking and need room for my pans and special goodies. If cooking isn't a hobby for you, maybe you need the extra cabinet space that can be used for storage for crafts or a home office. Maybe the kitchen table also needs to be used as an office or craft area or desk. Each of these will affect the design and layout of your space.

Placing the Kitchen

Think about where you want your kitchen to be located in your skoolie. I always like my kitchen to be on the side with the door. This way, when I am washing dishes, I can see what is going on in the campsite instead of the ugly campsite hookups.

Are you going to need a pantry?

Will you have upper cabinets or just have a shelf?

Are you buying prefab cabinets or making custom cabinets?

How much countertop space do you want?

Do you need a fixed table or one you store away?

Where will you place the trash can?

Where will you place the recycling bin?

Where will you place the compost bin?

Do you want upper cabinets?

Appliances and Equipment

Think about all the appliances and devices you will need in your skoolie. Take the time to notice what kitchen appliances you use that you would prefer not to do without. For example, my coffee pot, Instant Pot, and George Foreman Evolve are some of my favorites. What do YOU need in your kitchen area beside pots, pans, and food?

Take a look at the appliances and equipment that you use now and write down their measurements and the amp/watts of each appliance and device in the space provided in this chapter. (A list that includes all your electronic devices is not only helpful when planning your floor plan—it will also be useful when you're wiring your bus for power.)

Take some time to think about where the refrigerator, stove, water heater, freshwater tank, computers, and everything else will go. Once the list is complete, determine how much space each item is going to need and where it will be placed.

Do you want a stove top or stove/oven?

Will you have a propane or electric stove?

How large of a refrigerator do you need?

Do you want a tall refrigerator or undermount?

Will you have a propane, electric, or DC refrigerator?

Will you have a washer/dryer?

Where will you place the coffee pot? Or do you need a coffee/wine bar?

Appliance List

Appliance	Measurements	Watts/AMPS	Purchased At	Link

Standard Kitchen Measurements

Sink Base Cabinet:
 36" x 34.5" x 24" (W/L x H x D)
Single bowl drop-in:
 21"- 33" x 15"- 22" x 7"- 10" (L x W x D)
Double bowl drop-in:
 14"- 33" x 18"- 22" x 6"- 10" (L x W x D)
Drawer Cabinet:
 18" x 34.5" x 24" (W x H x D)
Custom Pantry:
 18" x 34.5" (W x D) (Made to fit the height of the bus.)
Upper Kitchen Cabinets (above sink area):
 12" deep to the top of windows
Upper Kitchen Shelf:
 12" deep, Custom length
Flip-up Table: 3' 6" x 1' 6" (W x D)

Appliances:

RV Stove:
 20.25" x 16" x 17.75" (W x H x D)
Stove/Oven:
 20" x 42" x 24.5" (W x H x D)
Washer/Dryer Combo:
 23.4" x 33.5" x 25.5" (W x H x D)
Refrigerator (Apt Size):
 10-11 cu - 24.5" x 62" x 28.5" (W x H x D)
Single door under mount refrigerator:
 23-24" x 33-35" x 24-25" (W x H x D)
Double door under mount refrigerator:
 34.25" x 35.5" x 23 - 25.13"; (H x W x D)
Microwave:
 14-20" x 12-20" x 9-12" (L x W x H)

CHAPTER 11
The Bedrooms

When designing your bedroom, close your eyes and imagine yourself relaxing after a long day of adventuring. What do you want to be nearby? How do you want your space to look and feel? What are the features that are going to make your life easier? Below, I will ask you several questions that will help you complete a thorough bedroom design for your floor plan.

Do you want a cabinet on each side of the bed, or are you going to save space and crawl over your partner to get out of bed?

What bedroom windows are you leaving and which ones will you cover up?

Do you want room on the sides of the bed to walk around or would you prefer having extra storage space?

Are you going to have accent lights? Maybe DC lights?

Do you need a DC plug in the bedroom?

How much privacy do you need?

Do you want a closet or storage in the master bedroom?

Will you need a "kid's room"?

Do you need a closet or toy storage in a kid's room?

Are you going to have a TV in the master bedroom?

Do you want bathroom access from the master bedroom?

Positioning the Bed

The bed will be the center piece of your bedroom. It's important to spend some time thinking about exactly where you want it to be and how you can use your space as wisely as possible.

Centered Bed: When positioning the bed in the center, it allows for easy access to both sides of the bed. In this position, there is room to build storage boxes, nightstands, or even install a closet on each side of the bed. You'll also have easy access to the storage underneath the bed via the side or foot of the bed. If the bus has the extra room, this is the way to go. A queen and king bed will work in this centered position but will only leave you a foot or less on each side of the bed.

Side Bed: A side bed is a bed that is positioned on one side of the bus. It can be a twin bed or larger. This works well to break up the center isle design. The underneath storage can be accessed via the foot of the bed or via the side of thebed. When two people share this bed, the inside person has to crawl over the other person or scoot off the end of the bed to get out.

Wall-to-Wall Bed: This bed stretches the width of the bus, meaning the head of the bed is on the right or left with the feet extending to the opposite side.

Depending on the size of your mattress, there may be extra inches at the foot or head of the bed. There are creative ways to use this space for storage, too. When two people are sleeping on the bed, the person lying next to the wall has to crawl over the person on the outside edge. If you can live with that, placing the bed in this position saves floor space. In a short bus, this is the best option for a full-size bed.

Will you bring in a bed or build one?

Do you want storage underneath the bed?

Which way do you want your bed to face? (This will determine what you see first thing in the morning.)

Do you want a cabinet on each side of the bed, or are you going to save space and crawl over your partner to get out of bed?

Where will you place the head of the bed?

Are you willing to crawl over a person to get in and out of bed?

Do you want room on the sides of the bed to walk around, or would you prefer having extra storage space?

How many people do you need to sleep in your skoolie?

Do you want a closet or storage in the master bedroom?

The Height of the Bed

You also want to decide how high you want your bed off the floor. This is going to affect the clearance over the bed and also determine how much storage space you have underneath. If you place an electric hot water heater under the bed, the standard bed height is 25 inches from the floor to the board the mattress sits on. If you don't put the water heater there, the standard is 16 inches off the floor.

How high off the floor do you want the bed?

How thick is your mattress?

Will the height of the bed and the mattress cover part of a window?

What bedroom windows are you leaving and which ones will you cover up?

Standard Bedroom Measurements

King Mattress:
  76" x 79.5" (W x H)
Queen Mattress:
  60" x 79.5" (W x H)
Full Mattress:
  53" x 74.5" (W x H)
Skoolie Bunk Bed Mattress:
  72" x 3" x 28" (W x H x D)
King Bed Frame:
  76" x 80" (W x D)
Queen Bed Frame:
  60" x 80" (W x D)
Full-Size Bed Frame:
  54"x 75" (W x D)
Skoolie Bunk Beds:
  24"x 72" (W x D)
Bedroom Closets:
  24" x 24" (W x D)
Wheel Well Closets:
  3' 8" x 1' 10 ¼" (interior dimensions) (W x D)
Bedroom Upper Cabinets:
  Above Back Door: 8" deep, height dependent on bus
  Above Head of Bed: 12" deep to the top of windows

CHAPTER 12
The Living Area

The "living area" in a skoolie is a pretty fluid concept. You'll be living in the whole thing! But for the purposes of this section, I am going to ask you some questions designed to help you determine what you need and want to get out of the primary living space.

Will you buy a couch or build a custom one?

If you build a custom couch, will you install cup holders?

Does the couch need built-in storage? (See *Chapter 7: Storage*)

Does the couch need seat belts?

Do you want electric outlets near the couch?

Do you want a separate living area from the kitchen?

Do you need a couch to function as extra sleeping space?

Do you need a desk area?

Do you need upper cabinets above the couch?

Where will everyone sit on travel days?

Do you need a TV or video gaming equipment storage?

Will kids be playing inside your skoolie? If so, where?

Standard Measurements for the Living Area

Loveseat:

Loveseats vary in size from 4 to 6 feet wide and 28 to 30 inches deep.

(This is just for reference, as you will likely build one with custom dimensions.)

Couch:

Sofas vary in size from 6 to 8 feet wide and 32 to 40 inches deep.

(This is just for reference, as you will likely build one with custom dimensions.)

Futon:

74" x 38" x 35.4" (W x D x H)

Utility Closet for Solar:

1' x 1' 8" (W x D)

CHAPTER 13
Power

Now let's talk power. Believe it or not, the kind of power you choose to use in your skoolie is going to affect your floor plan. This is because different power sources will require different amounts of storage space.

When it comes to powering your converted school bus, there are several options to choose from. You could use electric, solar, generator, or battery power. Many people use more than one source of power. I will speak briefly about each of these, but electric power is by far the most standard form of power that people choose.

Solar

For people who are looking for an environmentally friendly bus, solar is the go-to option. If you go this route, you will need to decide where to place the solar panels. Also keep in mind that you will need to access the panels for cleaning, clearing snow or debris, and wiping off bird poop.

Generator

A generator is nice to have on a skoolie for many reasons. When the AC/heat unit is connected to the generator, it can be used while driving. It also serves as a great option if you're going to be off-grid. Generators come in different sizes, so you will need to decide what size you want and make sure you include the necessary storage space in your floor plan. It's important to pay attention to where the generator will be placed under the bus. This may or may not affect your tank placements.

Battery

The number of batteries you will need depends on the amount of power in use and how often you want to recharge the batteries. The DIY Skoolie Guide gives a thorough overview of how to calculate how many batteries you might need based on the amount of electricity you're expecting to use each day.

Electric

You might decide to only connect to shore power—or power that is supplied by an external source that you can connect your bus to. Most of the time, it is 120-volt power. No matter what option is chosen for the main power supply in the bus, interior wiring will need to be completed, receptacles and switches installed, and then everything must be connected to the main power option. If you're exclusively using shore power, you will still need to make room to store the RV Power Center, which is the power center where all your wires are going to run.

What power sources do you want in your bus?

Where are you going to store the solar batteries?

Do you need a utility closet for all power needs?

Do you need a generator installed? If so, where?

What type of lighting are you going to want? (i.e., accent, ceiling, bedside, etc.)

Where do you want/need electrical outlets?

Do you want exterior lights or outlets?

Do you need/want internet?

Where will you place the water pump switch?

Will you have water tank sensors? If so, where is the switch going to be placed?

What appliances are you going to bring into your skoolie? (Refer to the list you made in *Chapter 10: The Kitchen and Appliances*)

CHAPTER 14
Heating and Cooling

If you are not going to be to spend your winters in Florida and summers in South Dakota, then figuring out how to heat and cool your skoolie efficiently is a must. As with most things in a conversion, your choice is going to come down to where you plan on living and traveling in your bus and how much money you want to spend.

Now, when you are making this decision, you also need to think about where you are going to put your source of heat and air because this is definitely going to affect your floor plan. So, let's talk about some of the different options available to you.

Pro Tip: *Install window screens on your bus windows. Cross ventilation on a breezy spring day will cool an off-grid bus in a matter of minutes.*

Heating Options

Wood Stoves: Wood stoves are becoming more popular for school bus conversions. If you decide go this route, you will need to decide where you will place it on your floor plan. You will also need to install a chimney, which can be installed through the roof or window of the bus.

NOTE: Most insurance companies frown on wood stoves and will deny giving you a policy if they know your skoolie has one on board. (Find out more about how to properly insure, title, and register your bus with our online book *Cover Your Bus*, which you can find at DIYskoolieguide.com.)

Propane Heaters: Propane heaters are a common option for heating a skoolie due to the fact that some of the appliances already function off propane. If you go this route, you will want to make sure you have room to store extra propane tanks.

Space Heaters: Space heaters can be used as a supplemental heating option. You will have to store them when you are not using them. For a shorter bus, you could probably get away with using just one. On a 40-foot bus, you would need two or three space heaters. To heat your skoolie comfortably, you will need to set the heater on high to get the job done.

What type of heat are you going to need?

Where will you place the heater?

Cooling Options

Rooftop Units: Rooftop AC units are widely used in school bus conversions. For a 35-foot bus or longer, I recommend installing two units. Shorter buses can get away with just one unit. Either way these units will be mounted to the roof and can be installed in the emergency hatch. You do want to be conscious of where you put your interior doors so that they do not hit the ceiling assembly of the AC Unit.

When drawing your floor plan, you will need to decide on how many AC units your bus will need to keep it cool and decide on the BTUs (British Thermal Units) each of these units need to have.

There are many brands of AC units to choose from. Dometic, Atwood and Coleman are a couple that are popular. My preference is a Coleman AC unit because it has been around for years. Coleman stands behind its warranties, has excellent customer service, offers heat strips, and the product parts are easy to purchase and affordable.

Window Units: Window units are a great option if you are working on a smaller budget. Keep in mind that if your window unit is not secured well, you may want to remove it on travel days. No one wants to lose a window unit while going down the road. Thus, you will need to make sure you have the necessary storage room.

Portable or Stand-Alone Units: There are several portable or stand-alone options for AC in a skoolie. From my experience, this is NOT a great option. These take up a lot of space and have to be vented. Many have tried it, only to return the units and put in a window or rooftop unit.

What type of AC are you going to use?

Where are you going to place the AC units?

Where are you going to place the thermostat?

CHAPTER 15
Planning for Your Wellbeing

In this chapter, I am going to talk about some of the most important elements of your floor plan. What do you, your partner, and/or your kids need in the skoolie to stay healthy mentally, physically, emotionally, and spiritually? Earlier, I mentioned how important it was for me to have alone/coffee time each morning. It is important that your floor plan reflects those needs. Make space for the most important things in your skoolie—which are the people who are living in it!

Hobbies and Routines

What do you need in your life in order to stay mentally healthy? This would include hobbies. For instance, in addition to cooking, I love to read! I have to have a spot next to my bed where I can stack at least four books. I also want a shelf or storage cabinet to store my travel books. These take up about 10-12 inches of space.

What do you, your partner, and/or your kids need in the skoolie to stay healthy mentally?

What accommodations do you need to make for those needs?

Do your children need toy storage?

What habits or routines do you or your partner/family members have that you need to consider?

List any hobbies that require you to have designated storage or dedicated areas. Next to each one, note how much space you think you will need.

Physical and Medical Needs

Now think about your medical needs. If you or a family member has a special need, how are you going to accommodate that need? Do you need storage space for medical supplies? One of my daughters is a Type 1 diabetic. It is helpful in my skoolie if I have one 12" x 12" cabinet to store all of her insulin supplies.

What medical equipment do you need to accommodate?

How much space/storage does the equipment require?

How many amps/watts does each piece of equipment use?

Do you need to have childproof locks?

CHAPTER 16
The Extras

Now that we've covered the basics, let's fill in the holes with all the extras you will need in order to meet your needs, wants, and must-haves.

The Driver's Area

The driver's area, also called the dog house, is a sacred place. Someone is going to be spending a lot of time there, and you want to try to make it as comfortable and pleasant as possible. You also want to consider how you can repurpose this space when you're not traveling.

How is the entrance shaped? Will this affect the floor plan?

Do you want a closet or shelf in this area?

Are you keeping the handrail?

How are you finishing out the stairs?

Where will you store shoes?

Wall Hangings

Are there any items that you want to hang on the wall? You will want to add extra horizontal studs for these so that they are secured for travel days and when the kids are running through the skoolie.

Do you have a heavy mirror to hang?

Would you like to add a medicine cabinet?

Is there a favorite picture frame that you would love to include in your design?

List the items and dimensions of anything you will be hanging on the wall:

Your Four-Legged Family

Don't forget to include room for your four-legged family! In addition, you want to make sure you know where he/she will be kept safe during travel days. Also, when considering your heating and cooling system, be sure to take into consideration that your pet may be left inside the bus alone.

Will you need to make room for a crate?

If your pet loves to chew up things, do you need to have a pet-proof area when you are away?

Does your pet sleep with you, or will they need their own area?

Do you need a place for a litter box?

Where are you going to store pet food and supplies?

Does your dog need regular baths? If so, is this done in a tub or shower?

Will you use an outdoor shower?

What is the measurement of the dog crate?

Do you have a pet that needs room for a tank or cage? If so, list the measurements below.

Exterior Considerations

There are several exterior elements that you will want to incorporate into your design. Some of these will directly affect your floor plan, whereas others will be details you can add on later.

Do you need exterior storage?

Are you going to need a roof raise?

Are you going to have a roof deck?

Do you want an awning?

Do you want a backup camera or side view cameras?

What color will you paint the bus?

Will you add a logo on the outside of the bus?

Are you going to install a water spigot on the exterior?

CHAPTER 17
Design Your Skoolie Floor Plan

Good job! You've made your way through the entire planning process. You have thought about all of your wants, needs, and cannot-live-with-outs. You've taken the time to answer all of my probing questions. Now you're ready to start drafting your floor plan!

Step 1: Draw the Bus to Scale

As I mentioned, my personal favorite design tools are graph paper and a pencil. If you use this method, each square will represent 12 inches.

Begin by drawing a rectangle on the paper with the correct dimensions of your bus. When using a computer program or app, you can follow the same directions below to create your floor plan. (See *Standard Bus Dimensions* at the end of this chapter.)

Step 2: Mark Off the Wheel Wells

After drawing your rectangle according to scale, mark off the wheel wells in the bus. Again, each square in the graph paper equals one square foot.

Step 3: Determine Where You Will Mount Your Holding Tanks

Go under the bus to see where the holding tanks are going to fit. Pay attention to how you need to run your water lines for the tanks and be mindful of weight distribution.

Step 4: Place the Bathroom

Once you know where the water tanks are going to go, you can place the bathroom on your plan. In order to get the best dimensions, sit on a bucket where you want the toilet to be. Then, measure exactly how much space you will need in the bathroom.

Step 5: Add the Other Elements

Next, add the garage area, master bedroom, and any bunks you're going to put in.
Then, draw in your couch, table, and kitchen area.
Next, add in the space and areas you will need for your pets.
On the floor plan, note any area where you will need extra horizontal studs.
Reference the *Helpful Standard Measurements* PDF in the appendix section for dimensions when placing cabinets, couches, beds, etc.

Step 6: Add Finishing Touches

Now is the time to add the upper cabinets and make notes on the floor plan for the extras that you want to include. Add any cabinets or shelves that you will build in the driver's area. Don't forget to make sure your laundry basket and trashcan have a designated area.

Step 7: Look for Holes in Your Design

Finally, look at your space to see where there are any gaps. If you need a cabinet, closet, or a pantry, add it now. Look back through the workbook to make sure you have included everything in the design that is important to your physical, spiritual, emotional, and mental health.

Pro Tip: *When placing items in your bus, keep in mind weight distribution.*

Step 8: Revise Your Floor Plan as Necessary

Often, once I've finished the first floor plan or blueprint, I have to make another one. Maybe the couch would fit better on the other side of the bus. I might move the table or the closets. Just remember, if you move your bathroom or kitchen sink, you will want to go back under your bus and make sure there is room for gray and black tanks.

Make as many designs as you need to until you are comfortable with your entire layout.

Step 9: Adding Electric and Plumbing

Once the final plan is chosen and marked off with tape on the bus floor, now is the time to plan out the electrical and plumbing.

Be sure you include your bathroom vent, AC units, and ceiling and accent lighting.

When I draw out an electrical plan, I use the letters "L," "M," and "H" (low, medium, and high) to designate the outlet positions on the wall.

I like to include the placement of the thermostat, water pump switch, generator switch, any DC outlets, and all switches—even on the floor plan.

Decide which wall you will use to place your light switch. I am right-handed and usually have the doors open into a room. The doorknob would be on the right andthe door would open to the left wall. Thus, I put the light switch on the right. You don't want the door to open to the left and the switch be located behind the door.

I do my best to keep the AC thermostat, water pump switch, and any kitchen light switches in the same area. Consolidating switches keeps the walls open for decorating. In my opinion, I find it aggravating when I want to hang a photo or a shelf on the wall and there is switch in the way. Do you agree?

On your floor plan, be sure to include where you will place any exterior lights or outlets.

Low outlet ("L"): 14" from floor
Medium outlet ("M"): 41" from floor
High outlet ("H"): 53" from floor

On the plumbing plans, I show where the freshwater tanks, water pump, washer/dryer, and plumbing will be placed. Be sure to include where the vent pipe will be placed and the compost toilet vent will be installed. In addition, I include where the exterior freshwater and city water inlets will be located, as well as any outdoor spigots.

If you are interested in having a consult about creating your floor plan, contact support@DIYskoolieguide.com for pricing and more information.

Conclusion

Once you've settled on the floor plan that you are going to use, or if you just want to bounce your ideas off of other skoolie owners and fans, join us in the *Four Wheels And A Bra Facebook Group* and share!

Standard Bus Dimensions

Buses are measured bumper to bumper as follows:

40-foot front engine bus* → approximately 36-foot of convertible space
35-foot front engine bus* → approximately 31 feet ofconvertible space
37-foot conventional bus → approximately 27 feet of convertible space
30-foot conventional bus → approximately 21 feet of convertible space

* A rear engine bus with the same dimensions might give you one foot of extra space. It really depends on the bus. I suggest using the same footage as a front engine for now.

Width

The width of the bus will be determined by how you build your walls. I prefer to frame out the bus and add insulation. Therefore, most of the buses are between 7.2 feet and 7.5 feet wide inside. This measurement is important because you want to make sure you place your doors and appliances so that the doors open freely.

APPENDIX

Questions to Ask Yourself Before Planning a Skoolie Design

Here is a comprehensive list of questions to answer BEFORE you begin planning your skoolie floor plan. Some of these questions will not directly affect the actual floor plan design, but they will affect the overall design of the skoolie. So, it is still important to think about these questions now.

If you haven't already done so, I recommend that you go through my short, free course *School Bus to Home on Wheels*, which you can find at DIYskoolieguide.com. In that course, I walk you through a series of "why" questions that will help you determine the purpose of your bus and make sure your floor plan is in alignment with your bigger dreams.

The Purpose of Your Skoolie:

What is your purpose and plan for your skoolie? Will it be for full-time travel or used as a weekend camper?

Where will you visit and at what time of year?

How do you need your skoolie to function?

What are your priorities? (i.e., room for pets, size of beds, a place to work, etc.)

How would you like it to flow? (i.e., center aisle or side aisle)

What is your style? Does it affect the layout?

Is there special equipment or gadgets that you can't live without?

What are the "must-haves" in your skoolie?

Do you need to have a child-proof area?

General Questions:

How tall is the tallest person who will be living/traveling in your skoolie?

Do you have any special storage needs, such as for activity equipment, work supplies, or medical supplies?

Do you need to leave any windows for cross-ventilation?

Where are your egress exits?

Are you going to have frequent guests?

Will you need space-saving options?

Are you repurposing any furniture?

Where are the wheel wells?

Are there any metal structures under the bus that will impede the design? These would include things such as metal ribs, on-board AC, and the battery box.

Building Materials:

What type of building materials will you use for your studs? The studs can be made out of 2x4s ripped down to 2x2s, or you can buy 2x2s or 2x3s. Whichever one you choose, it will affect the floor plan due to the width of the stud.

What type of material will you use on the walls? If you use lauan plywood, it is ¼ inch thick. If you use tongue and groove boards, the thickness will depend on the boards you choose.

What flooring will you use? The depth of the flooring will affect the clearance from the ceiling to the floor.

Exterior:

Do you want to keep the back door accessible?

Does your bus have a side door? Do you want to utilize it in the design?

Are you keeping the bus door or using an RV Door?

Are you keeping the bus windows or replacing them with RV Windows?

Do you need exterior storage?

Are you going to need a roof raise?

Are you going to have a roof deck?

Do you want an awning?

Do you want a backup camera or side view cameras?

What color will you paint the bus?

Will you add a logo on the outside of the bus?

Are you going to install a water spigot on the exterior?

Bedroom Space:

How many people do you need to sleep?

Will you bring in a bed or build one?

Do you want storage underneath the bed?

How high off the floor do you want the bed?

How thick is your mattress?

Will the height of the bed and the mattress cover part of a window?

Where will you place the head of the bed?

Do you want to have to crawl over a person to get in and out of bed?

Do you want room on the sides of the bed to walk around or would you prefer having extra storage space?

How much privacy do you need?

What windows are you leaving, and which ones will you cover up?

Do you want a closet or storage in the master bedroom?

Do you need a closet or toy storage in a kid's room?

How much space, if any, do you want in the back of the bus?

Are you going to have a TV in the master bedroom?

Are you going to have accent lights? Maybe DC lights?

Do you need a DC plug in the bedroom?

Bathroom Space:

Do you want a tub/shower or just a shower? (Be sure to allow room for your shower valve.)

What size shower/tub do you want? What materials will you use for the tub/shower area? (tile, tin, decorative tiles, RV surround, etc.)

Where do you want to place the bathroom? On one side of the bus or across both sides?

What type of toilet are you going to use?

How much space do you need to get ready in the mornings?

What size vanity do you need?

Where are you going to place the mirror?

Will the light be in the ceiling or over the mirror?

Do you want a trashcan in the bathroom?

Will you leave a window in the bathroom?

Are you going to install a bathroom vent fan?

How many electrical outlets will you need in the bathroom?

Do you need a storage or linen closet?

Where will you store dirty laundry?

Kitchen Space:

Do you want a stove top or stove/oven?

Will you have a propane or electric stove?

How large of a refrigerator do you need?

Do you want a tall refrigerator or undermount?

Will you have a propane, electric, or DC refrigerator?

What appliances do you need? Washer/dryer? Microwave?

Where will you place the coffee pot? Or do you need a coffee/wine bar?

How much countertop space do you want?

Do you need a fixed table or one you store away? Are you going to need a pantry?

Do you want upper cabinets, or will you just use shelves?

Are you buying prefab cabinets or making custom cabinets?

Where will you place the trash can? Recycling bin? Compost bin?

Living Area:

Do you want a separate living area from the kitchen?

Do you need a couch to function as extra sleeping space?

Will you buy a couch or build a custom one?

If you build a custom couch, have you thought about installing cup holders?

Do you want a water filtration system?

Does the couch need storage built in?

Where will everyone sit on travel days?

Does the couch need seat belts?

Do you need a desk area?

Do you need a TV or video gaming equipment storage?

Do you need upper cabinets above the couch?

Where are the kids going to play inside the skoolie?

Do you want electric outlets near the couch?

Driver's Area:

How is the entrance shaped?
Will this affect the floor plan?
Do you want a closet or shelf in this area?
Are you keeping the handrail?
How are you finishing out the stairs?
Where will you store shoes?

Power:

What appliances do you use now that you will bring into your skoolie?
    Where will you store these?
    What are the amps/watts?
    Where do you want/need electrical outlets?
What power sources do you want in your bus? (i.e., solar, propane,electric, etc.)
Where are you going to store the solar batteries?
Do you need a utility closet for all power needs?
What type of lighting are you going to want? (i.e., accent, ceiling, bedside,etc.)
Are you wanting exterior lights or outlets?
Do you need/want internet?
Are you needing a generator installed? If so, where?
Where will you place the water pump switch?
Will you have water tank sensors? If so, where is the switch going to be placed?

Heating and Cooling:

What type of AC are you going to use? (i.e., mini-split, roof top, stand-alone unit, etc.)
Where are you going to place the AC units? Thermostat?
What type of heat are you going to need? (i.e., wood, propane, diesel, electric,etc.)
Where will you place the heater?

Plumbing/Tanks:

How much freshwater will you need?
    Where are you going to store the tank?
How many gray tanks do you need?
    Where will they be placed under the bus?
Will you need a black tank?
    Where will it be placed under the bus?
What size hot water heater do you want?
    Where are you going to put it?
Do you want any outdoor spigots?
Are you going to install an outdoor shower?

Helpful Standard Measurements

Standard Bathroom Measurements:

Bathroom Side-Aisle:
Large: 6' 6 ½" x 4' 4½" (W x D)
Standard: 5' 9"x 3' ½" (W x D)
Bathroom, both sides of the bus:
6' 7" x 2' 9 ½" (W x D)
Wet-bath:
3' 5 ½" x 2' (W x D)
Compost or RV Toilet:
24" x 24" (W x D)
Vanity (this can also be custom designed):
18" x 34.5" x 24" or 24" x 24" x 34. 5" (W x H x D)
Vessel Sink:
13-16" x 13-16" x 4-6" (L x W x H)
White Porcelain Rectangle Sink:
14"-17" x 18"-21" x 5-¾" (L x W x D)
White Ceramic Rectangular Vessel Bathroom Sink:
18-23" x 14.25" x 4.31" (L xW x D)
RV Shower:
40" x 24" or 36" x 36" (W x D)
RV Tub:
40" x 24" (W x D)

Standard Kitchen Measurements:

Sink Base Cabinet:
36" x 34.5" x 24" (W/L x H x D)
Single bowl drop-in:
21"- 33" x 15"- 22" x 7"- 10" (L x W x D)
Double bowl drop-in:
14"- 33" x 18"- 22" x 6"- 10" (L x W x D)
Drawer Cabinet:
18" x 34.5" x 24" (W x H x D)
Custom Pantry:
18" x 34.5" (W x D) (Made to fit the height of the bus.)
Upper Kitchen Cabinets (above sink area):
12" deep to the top of windows
Upper Kitchen Shelf:
12" deep. Custom length
Flip-up Table: 3' 6" x 1' 6" (W x D)

Appliances:

RV Stove:
    20.25" x 16" x 17.75" (W x H x D)

Stove/Oven:
    20" x 42" x 24.5" (W x H x D)

Washer/Dryer Combo:
    23.4" x 33.5" x 25.5" (W x H x D)

Refrigerator (Apt Size):
    10-11 cu - 24.5" x 62" x 28.5" (W x H x D)

Single door under mount refrigerator:
    23-24" x 33-35" x 24-25" (W x H x D)

Double door under mount refrigerator:
    34.25" x 35.5" x 23 - 25.13"; (H x W x D)

Microwave:
    14-20" x 12-20" x 9-12" (L x W x H)

Standard Bedroom Measurements:

King Mattress:
      76" x 79.5" (W x H)

Queen Mattress:
    60" x 79.5" (W x H)

Full Mattress:
    53" x 74.5" (W x H)

Skoolie Bunk Bed Mattress
    72" x 3" x 28" (W x H x D)

King Bed Frame:
    76" x 80" (W x D)

Queen Bed Frame:
    60" x 80" (W x D)

Full-Size Bed Frame:
    54"x 75" (W x D)

Skoolie Bunk Beds:
    24"x 72" (W x D)

Bedroom Closets:
    24" x 24" (W x D)

Wheel Well Closets:
    3' 8" x 1' 10 ¼" (interior dimensions) (W x D)

Bedroom Upper Cabinets:
    Above Back Door: 8" deep, height dependent on bus
    Above Head of Bed: 12" deep to the top of windows

Standard Measurements for the Living Area:

Loveseat:

Loveseats vary in size from 4 to 6 feet wide and 28 to 30 inches deep.

(This is just for reference, as you will likely build one with custom dimensions.)

Couch:

Sofas vary in size from 6 to 8 feet wide and 32 to 40 inches deep.

(This is just for reference, as you will likely build one with custom dimensions.)

Futon:

74" x 38" x 35.4" (W x D x H)

Utility Closet for Solar:

1' x 1' 8" (W x D)

Bus Dimensions

40-foot front engine bus → approximately 36-foot of convertible space

35-foot front engine bus → approximately 31 feet ofconvertible space

37-foot conventional bus → approximately 27 feet of convertible space

30-foot conventional bus → approximately 21 feet of convertible space

- The bus' length is measured from bumper to bumper.
- A rear engine bus might give you one foot of extra space. It really depends on the bus. I suggest using the same footage as a front engine for now.
- The width of the bus will be determined by how you build your walls. I prefer to frame out the bus and add insulation. Therefore, most of the buses are between 7.2 feet and 7.5 feet wide inside. This measurement is important because you want to make sure you place your doors and appliances so that the doors open freely.

Driver's Area:

Shoe Cubby at the entrance: Custom

Driver's shelf: Custom

Water Tanks:

Fresh Water: 46 gal

Gray Water: 34 gal 23.75" x 8" x 55.75" (W x D x L)

(You can purchase smaller or larger ones depending on the space you have under the bus.)

Standard Door openings:

24" to 28" wide

AC Units & Vent Fans:

Usually a 14" x 14" opening on the ceiling

RV Dealer Notes

What I liked:

What I didn't like:

Measurements taken

Furniture to Reuse or Recycle

Item	Measurements	Room Placement	Notes

Appliance List

Appliance	Measurements	Watts/AMPS	Purchased At	Link